TOOLS FOR CAREGIVERS

- **F&P LEVEL:** C
- **WORD COUNT:** 33
- **CURRICULUM CONNECTIONS:** machines

Skills to Teach

- **HIGH-FREQUENCY WORDS:** a, big, for, has, in, is, it, the
- **CONTENT WORDS:** back, box, dirt, drives, dump(s), goes, lifts, more, truck, wheels
- **PUNCTUATION:** exclamation point, periods
- **WORD STUDY:** /k/, spelled ck (*back*, *truck*); long /e/, spelled ee (*wheels*); short /u/ (*dump*, *truck*)
- **TEXT TYPE:** information report

Before Reading Activities

- Read the title and give a simple statement of the main idea.
- Have students "walk" through the book and talk about what they see in the pictures.
- Introduce new vocabulary by having students predict the first letter and locate the word in the text.
- Discuss any unfamiliar concepts that are in the text.

After Reading Activities

Ask readers what vowel sound is in both "dump" and "trucks." Then ask them to name other words with the short /u/ vowel sound, such as "bug" and "cup." Write their answers on the board.

Tadpole Books are published by Jump!, 5357 Penn Avenue South, Minneapolis, MN 55419, www.jumplibrary.com

Copyright ©2025 Jump. International copyright reserved in all countries. No part of this book may be reproduced in any form without written permission from the publisher.

Editor: Jenna Gleisner **Designer:** Emma Almgren-Bersie

Photo Credits: TFoxFoto/Shutterstock, cover, 2tr, 6–7; Maksim Safaniuk/Shutterstock, 1; SEVENNINE_79/Shutterstock, 2tl, 2br, 4–5; BGStock72/Shutterstock, 2ml, 8–9; Jumparound65/Dreamstime, 2mr, 12–13; Amy S. Myers/Dreamstime, 2bl, 10–11; m_albert/Shutterstock, 3; Lucian Coman/Shutterstock, 14–15; RobSt/Shutterstock, 16.

Library of Congress Cataloging-in-Publication Data
Names: Gleisner, Jenna Lee, author.
Title: Dump trucks / by Jenna Lee Gleisner.
Description: Minneapolis, MN: Jump!, Inc., [2025]
Series: Machines on the move | Includes index
Audience: Ages 3–6
Identifiers: LCCN 2024021024 (print)
LCCN 2024021025 (ebook)
ISBN 9798892135955 (hardcover)
ISBN 9798892135962 (paperback)
ISBN 9798892135979 (ebook)
Subjects: LCSH: Dump trucks—Juvenile literature.
Classification: LCC TL230.15 .G57 2025 (print)
LCC TL230.15 (ebook)
DDC 629.225—dc23/eng/20240510
LC record available at https://lccn.loc.gov/2024021024
LC ebook record available at https://lccn.loc.gov/2024021025

MACHINES ON THE MOVE
DUMP TRUCKS

by Jenna Lee Gleisner

TABLE OF CONTENTS

Words to Know	2
Dump It	3
Let's Review!	16
Index	16

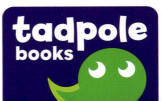

WORDS TO KNOW

box   dirt

drives   dumps

lifts   wheels

DUMP IT

A dump truck is big!

box

It has big wheels.

It has a big box.

Dirt goes in.

The truck drives.

The box lifts.

It dumps dirt.

It goes back for more.

LET'S REVIEW!

Dump trucks are big machines! What part of the machine is this?

INDEX

box 5, 11
dirt 7, 13
drives 9

dumps 13
lifts 11
wheels 4